# IRISH FAVORITES
## FOR ACCORDION

### ARRANGED BY GARY MEISNER

## CONTENTS

ISBN 978-1-4234-1347-9

HAL•LEONARD®
CORPORATION
7777 W. BLUEMOUND RD. P.O. BOX 13819 MILWAUKEE, WI 53213

In Australia Contact:
**Hal Leonard Australia Pty. Ltd.**
4 Lentara Court
Cheltenham, Victoria, 3192 Australia
Email: ausadmin@halleonard.com

Visit Hal Leonard Online at
**www.halleonard.com**

# THE BAND PLAYED ON

Words by JOHN E. PALMER
Music by CHARLES B. WARD

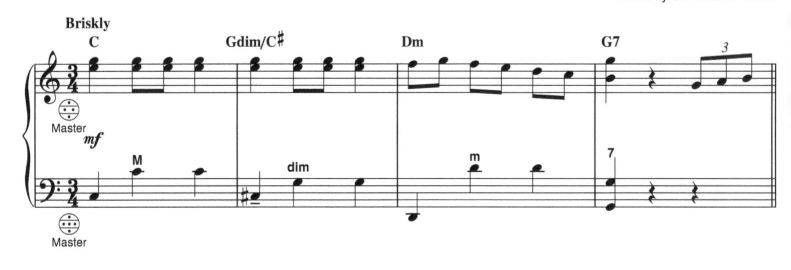

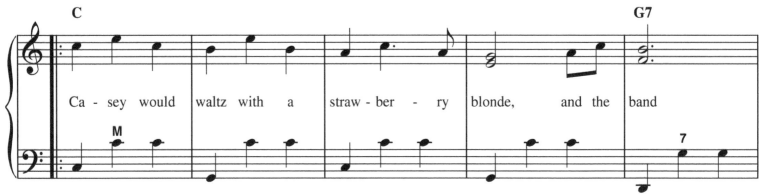

Ca - sey would waltz with a straw - ber - ry blonde, and the band

played on. He'd glide 'cross the floor with the

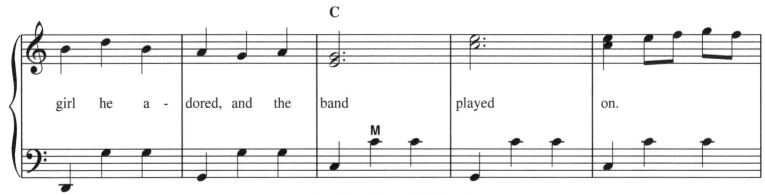

girl he a - dored, and the band played on.

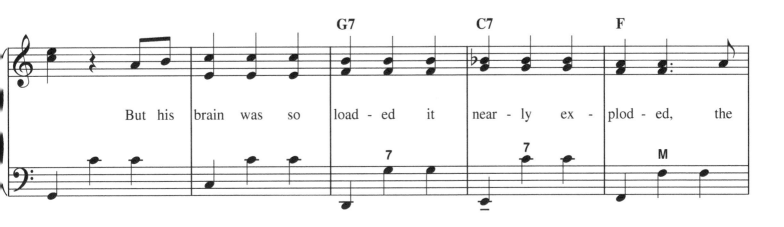

But his brain was so load-ed it near-ly ex-plod-ed, the

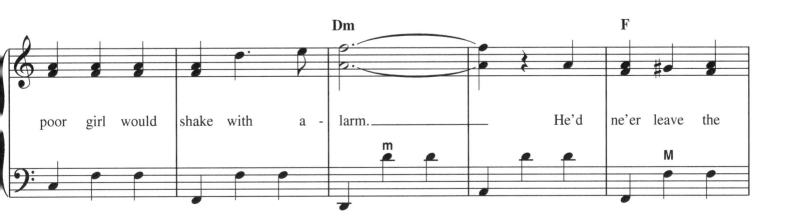

poor girl would shake with a - larm._____ He'd ne'er leave the

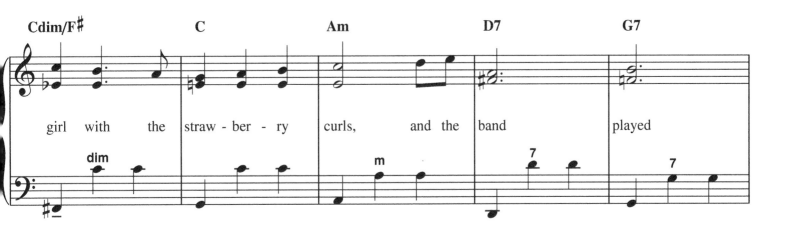

girl with the straw-ber-ry curls, and the band played

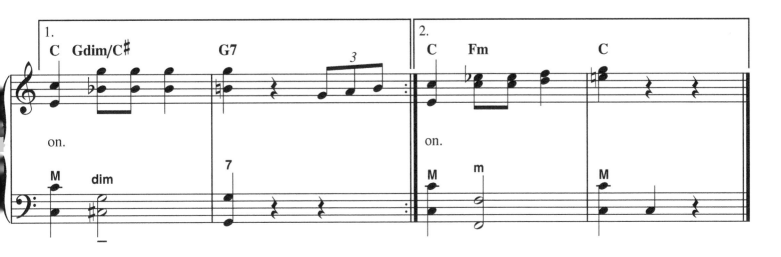

1. on.

2. on.

# BELIEVE ME, IF ALL THOSE ENDEARING YOUNG CHARMS

Words and Music by
THOMAS MOORE

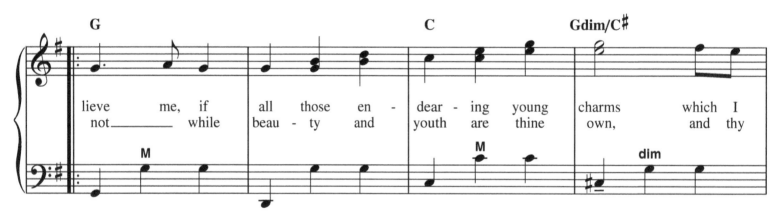

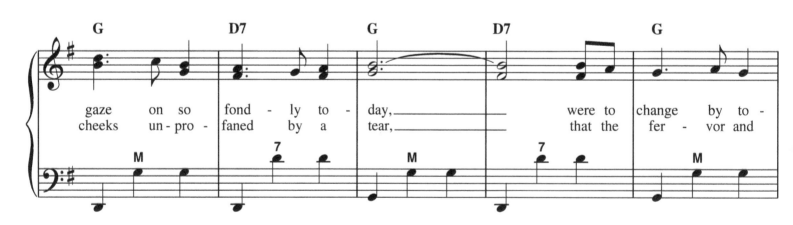

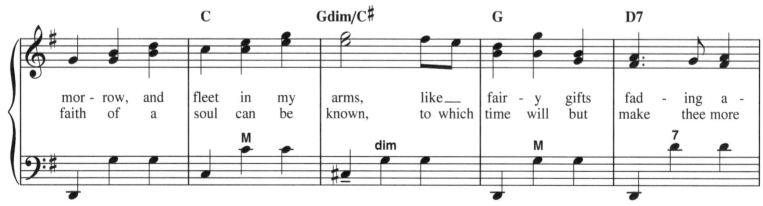

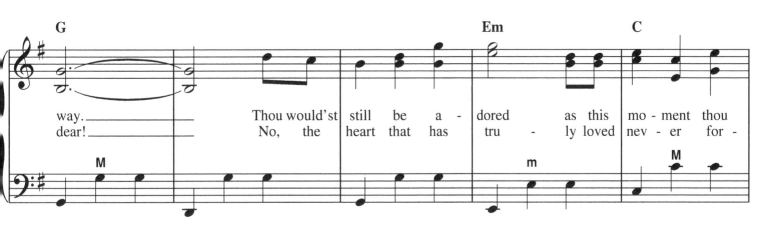

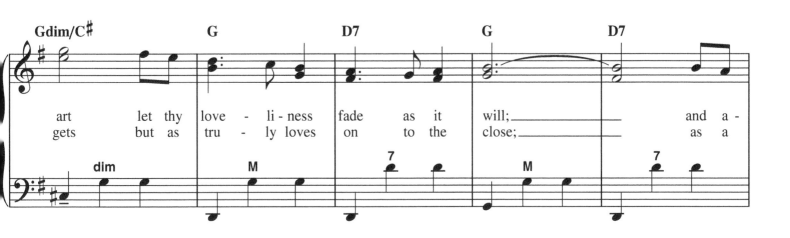

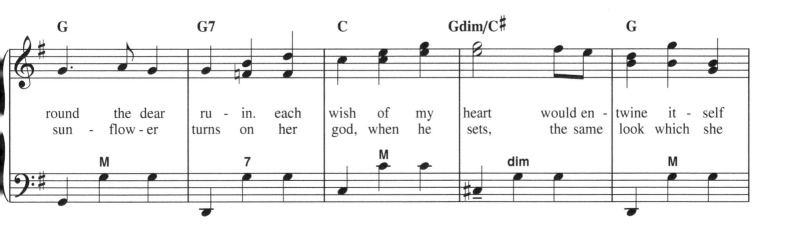

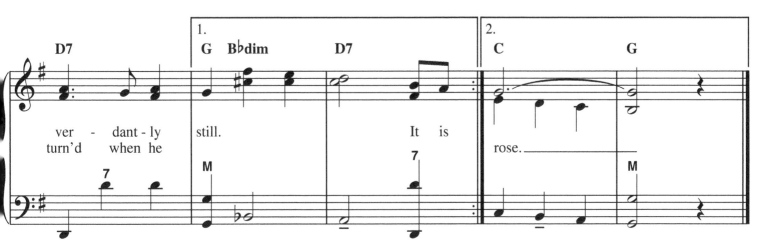

# DANNY BOY

### featured in the Television Series THE DANNY THOMAS SHOW

Words by FREDERICK EDWARD WEATHERLY
Traditional Irish Folk Melody

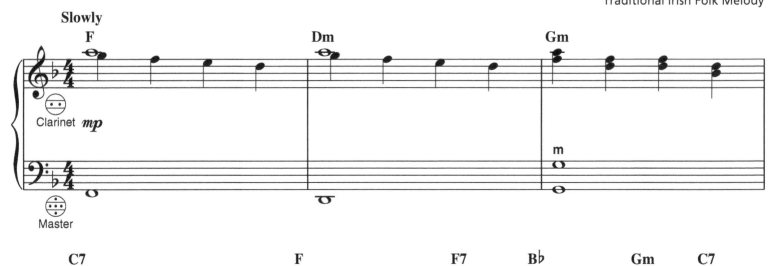

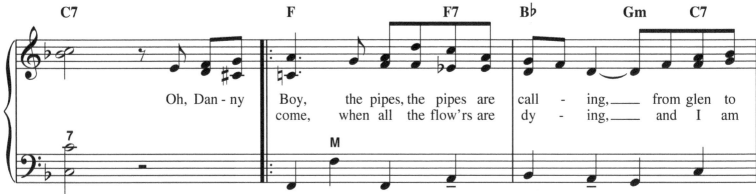

Oh, Dan - ny Boy, the pipes, the pipes are call - ing,___ from glen to
come, when all the flow'rs are dy - ing,___ and I am

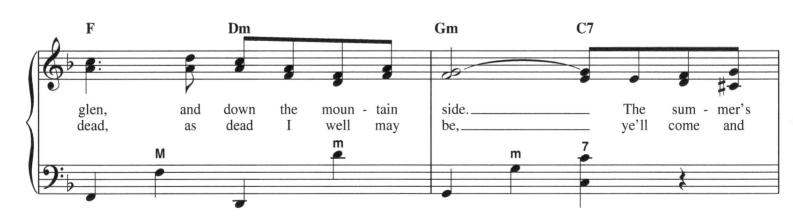

glen, and down the moun - tain side._____ The sum - mer's
dead, as dead I well may be,_____ ye'll come and

gone, and all the ros - es fall - ing,___ It's you, it's
find the place where I am ly - ing,___ and kneel and

you must go and I must
say an A - ve there for

# GARRYOWEN

Irish Folksong

# HARRIGAN

**from GEORGE M!**

Words and Music by
GEORGE M. COHAN

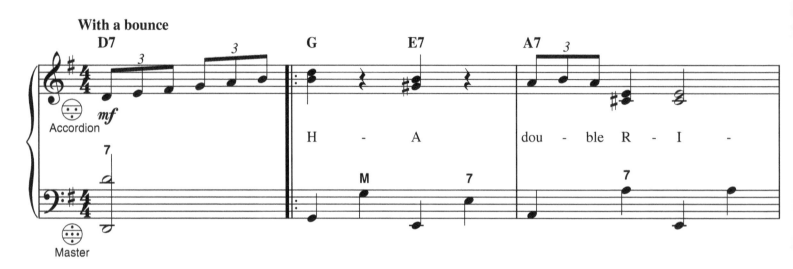

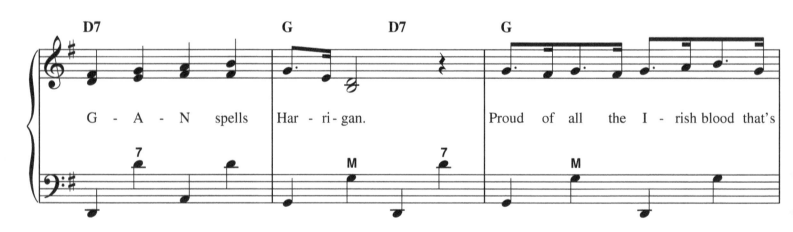

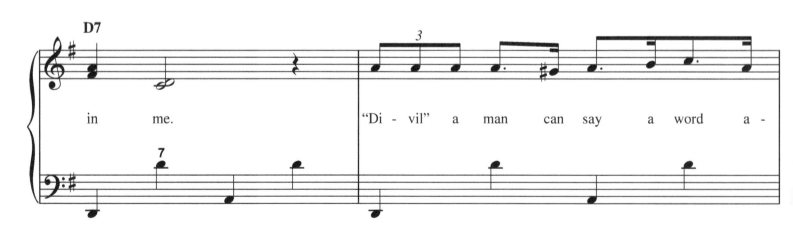

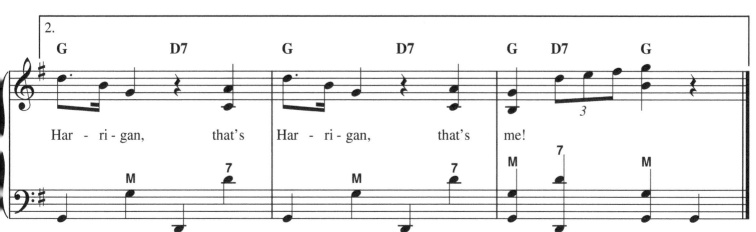

# I'LL TAKE YOU HOME AGAIN, KATHLEEN

Words and Music by
THOMAS WESTENDORF

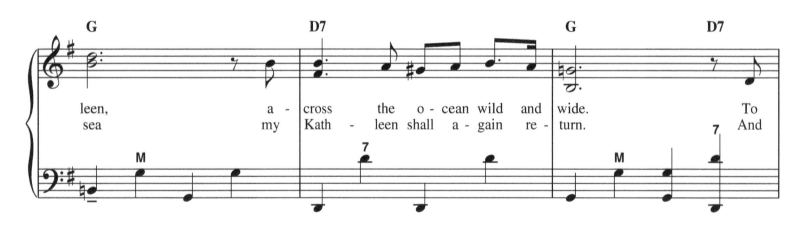

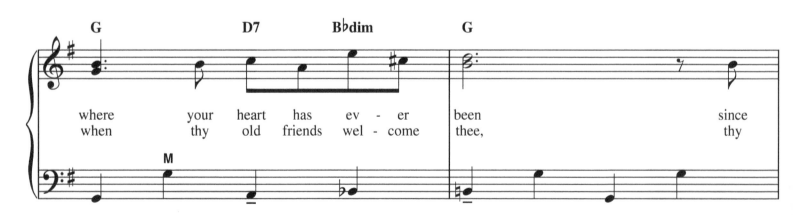

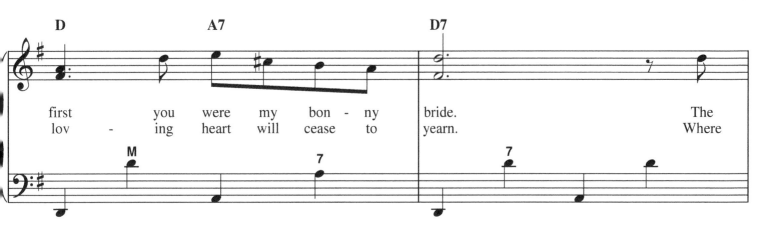

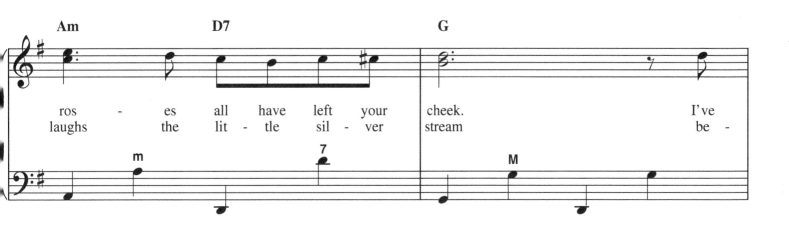

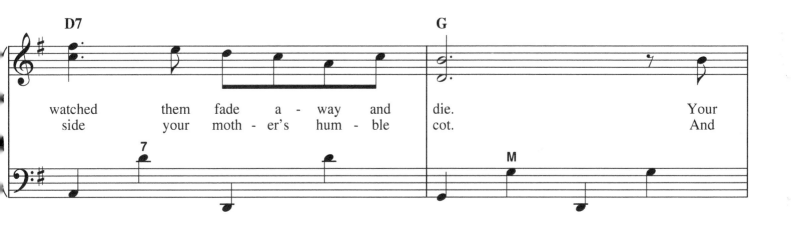

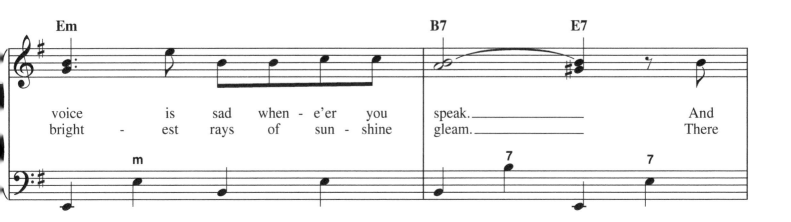

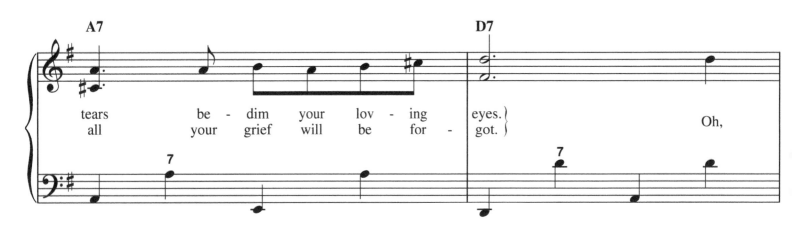

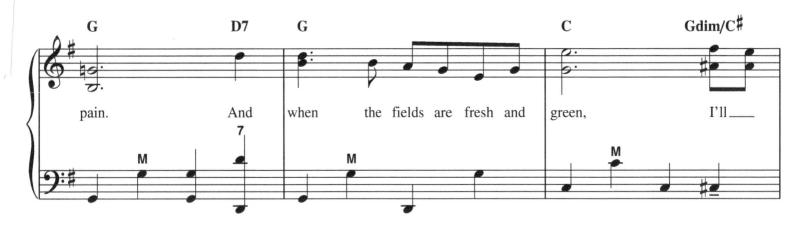

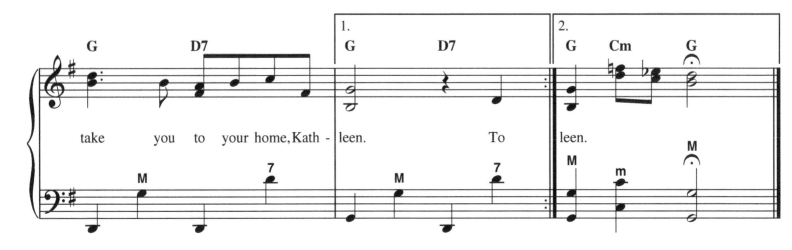

# McNAMARA'S BAND

Words by JOHN J. STAMFORD
Music by SHAMUS O'CONNOR

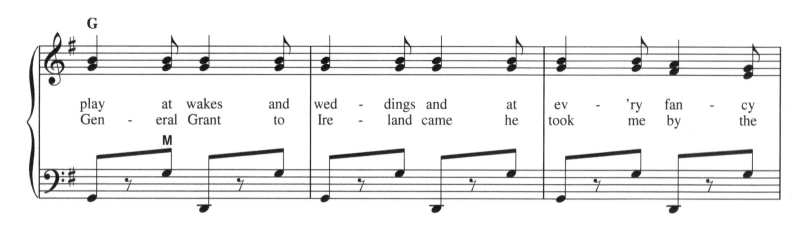

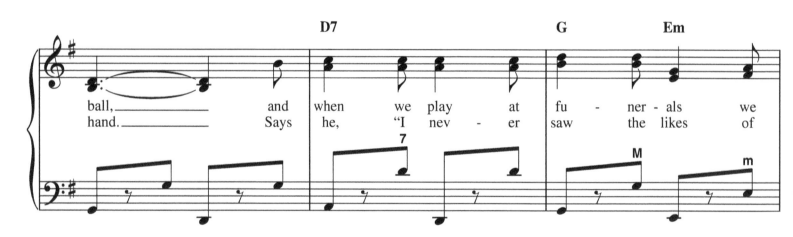

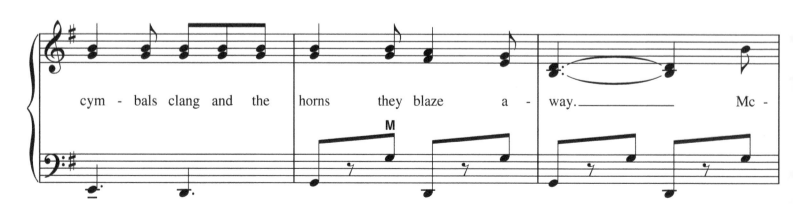

# THE IRISH WASHERWOMAN

Irish Folksong

# KERRY DANCE

By J.L. MOLLOY

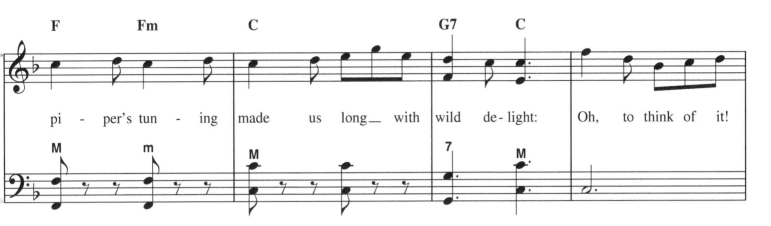

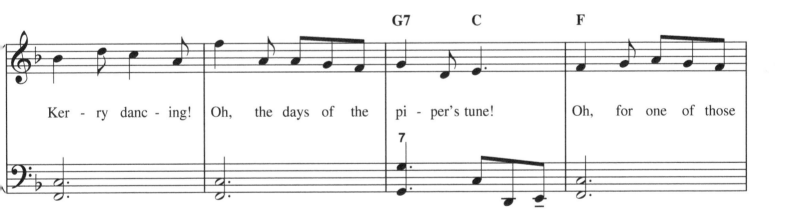

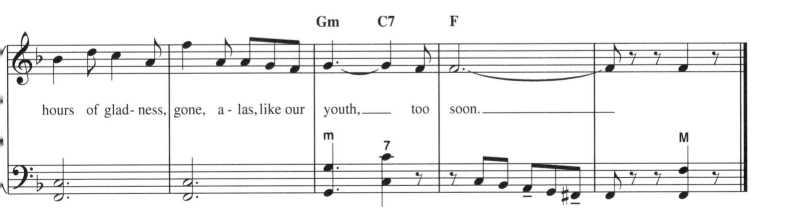

# LITTLE ANNIE ROONEY

Words and Music by
MICHAEL NOLAN

**With motion**

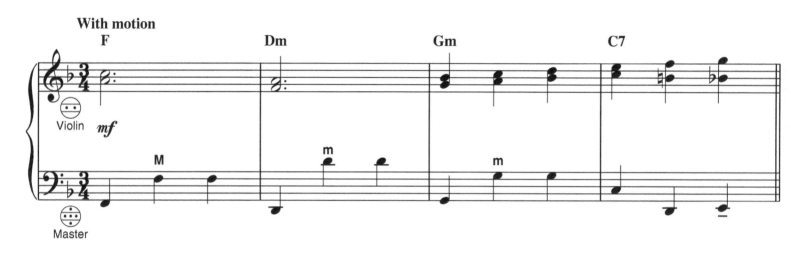

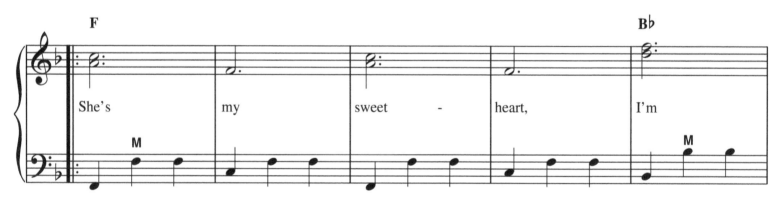

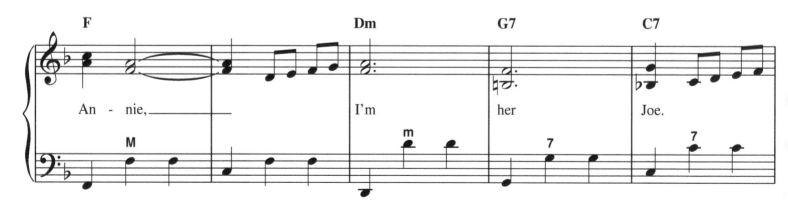

Soon we'll mar - ry

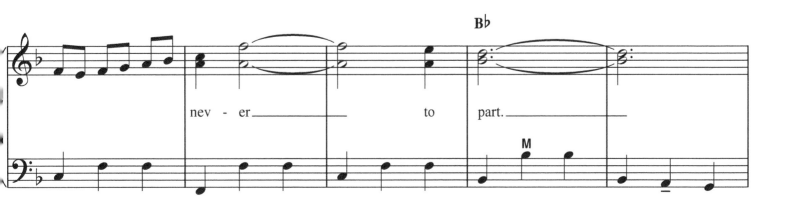

nev - er_____ to part._____

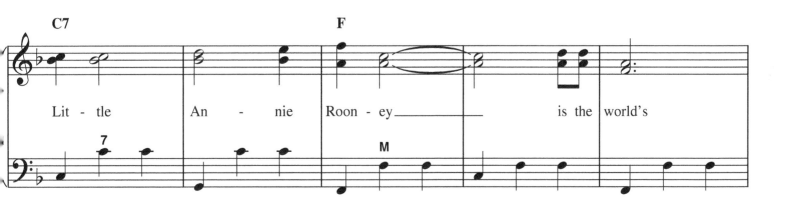

Lit - tle An - nie Roon - ey_____ is the world's

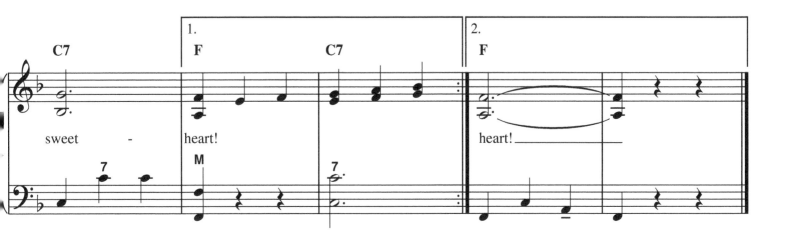

sweet - heart! heart!_____

# A LITTLE BIT OF HEAVEN

Words by ERNEST R. BALL
Music by J. KEIRN BRENAN

# MARY'S A GRAND OLD NAME

### from GEORGE M!
### from FORTY-FIVE MINUTES FROM BROADWAY

Words and Music by
GEORGE M. COHAN

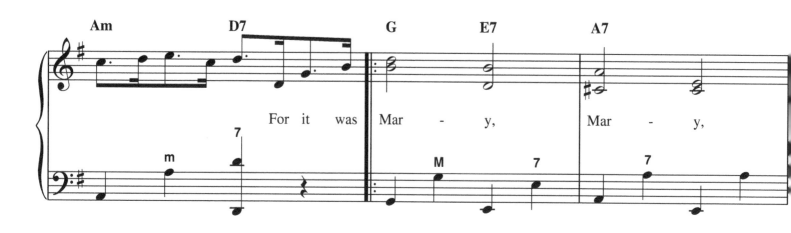

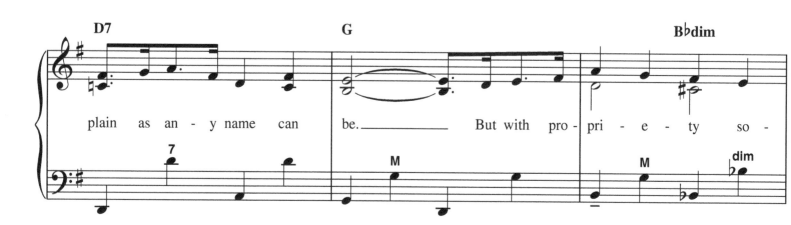

# MOLLY MALONE
## (Cockles & Mussels)

Irish Folksong

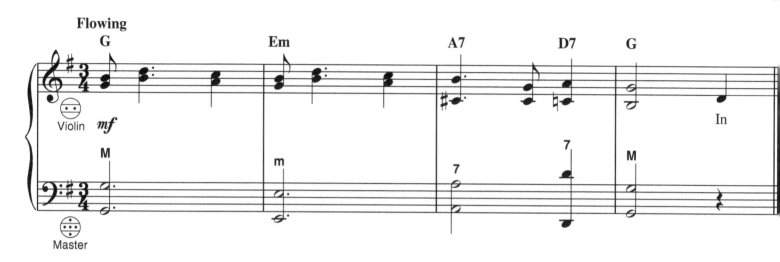

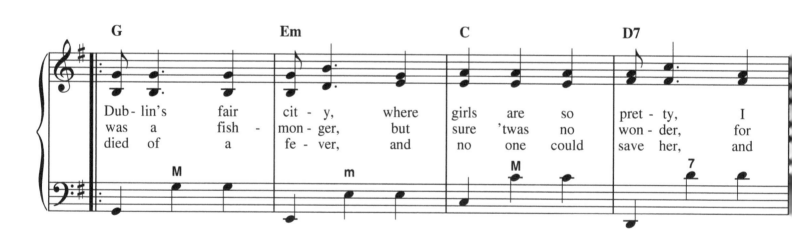

Dub- lin's fair cit - y, where girls are so pret - ty, I
was a fish - mon- ger, where but sure 'twas no won - der, for
died of a fe - ver, but and no one could save her, for and

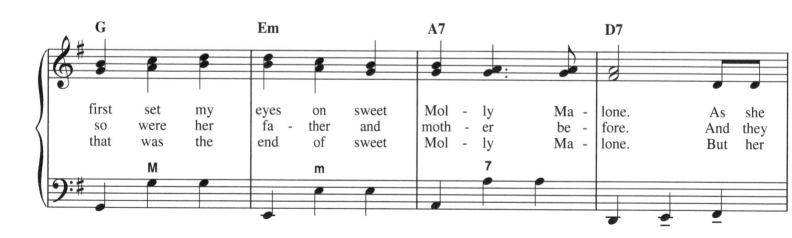

first set my eyes on sweet Mol - ly Ma - lone. As she
so were her fa - ther and moth - er be - fore. And they
that was her the end of sweet Mol - ly Ma - lone. But her

# MY WILD IRISH ROSE

Words and Music by
CHAUNCEY OLCOTT

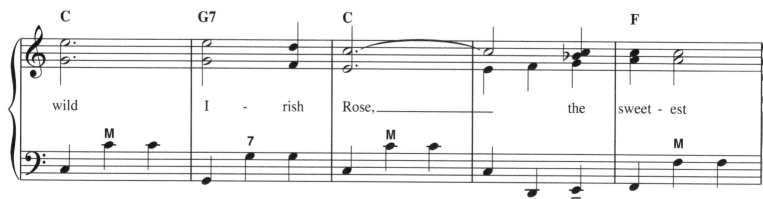

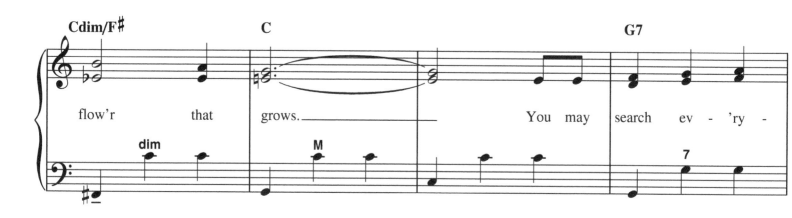

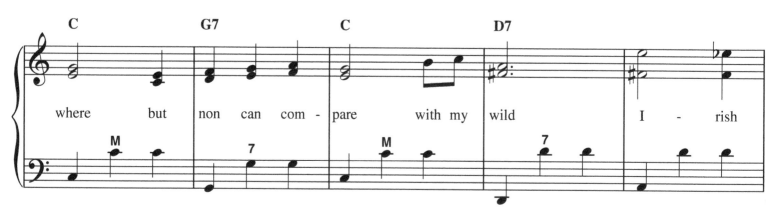

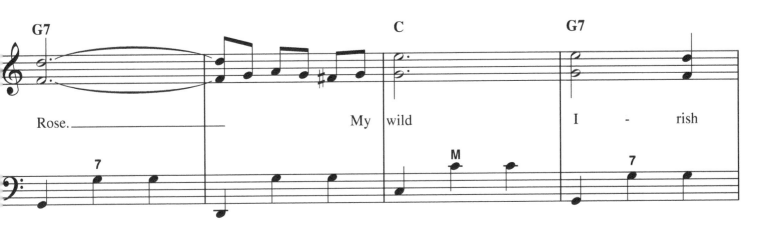

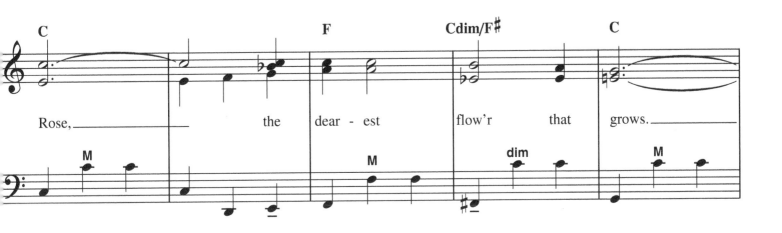

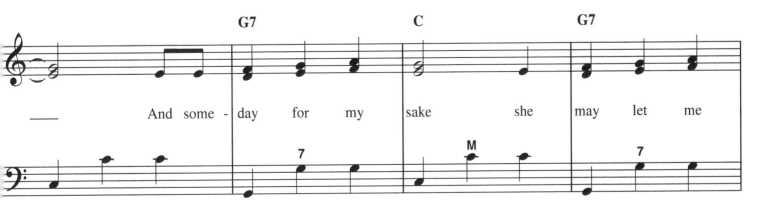

# PEG O' MY HEART

Words by ALFRED BRYAN
Music by FRED FISHER

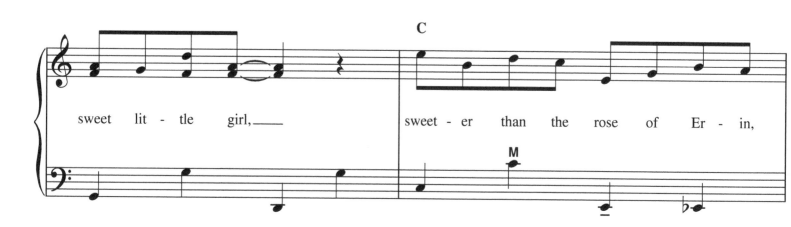

# SAILOR'S HORNPIPE

Sea Chantey

# TOO-RA-LOO-RA-LOO-RAL
### (That's an Irish Lullaby)
## from GOING MY WAY

Words and Music by
JAMES R. SHANNON

36

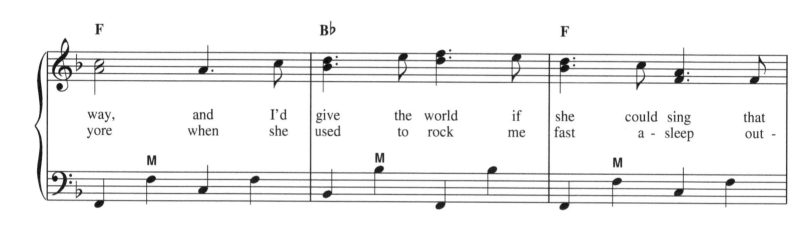

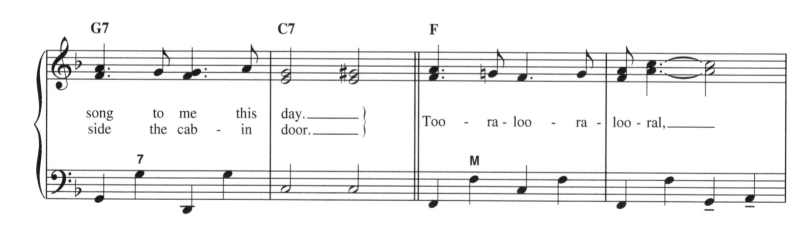

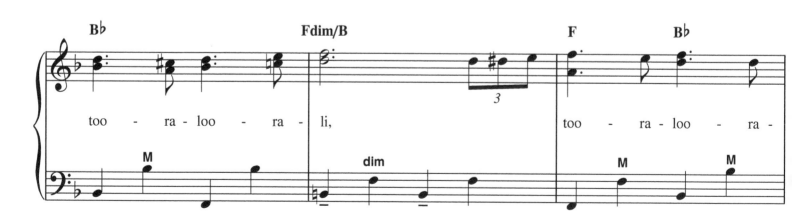

# SWEET ROSIE O'GRADY

Words and Music by
MAUDE NUGENT

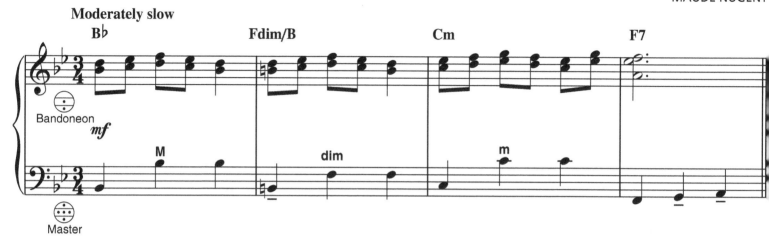

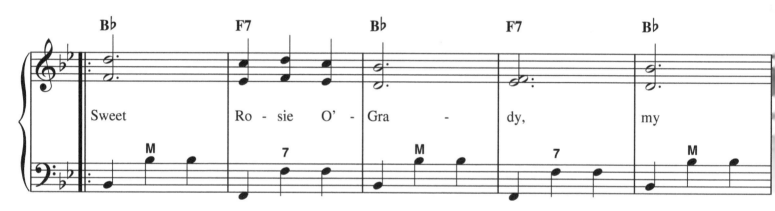

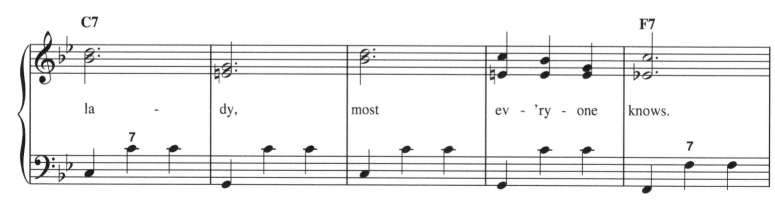

# TOURELAY, TOURELAY

Irish Folksong

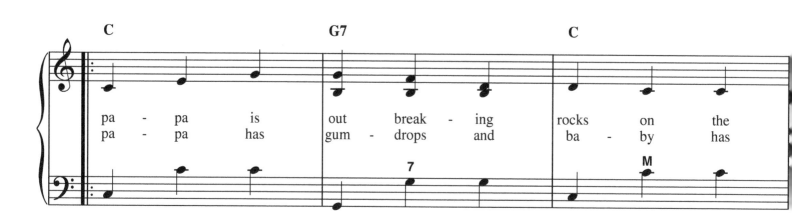

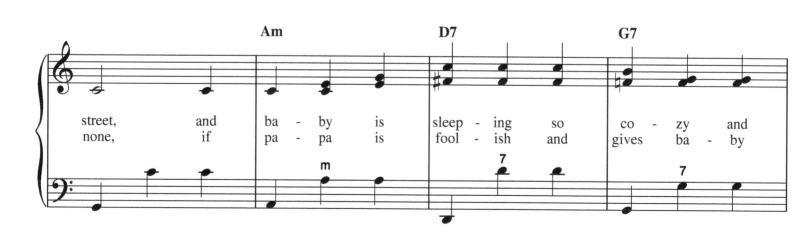

sweet. Oh, ba - by, don't cry now, but be ver - y
some, when four o' - clock comes and the child sleeps no

good and when pa - pa comes home he'll bring
more, then poor pa - pa stays up all night

you cig - a - root. } Tou - re - lay! Tou - re -
pac - ing the floor. }

lay! With my fil - la - ga du - sha, shin - a - ma

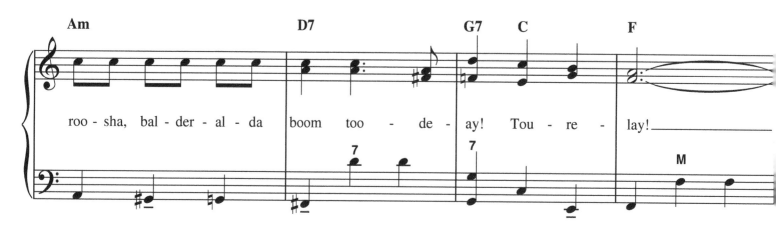

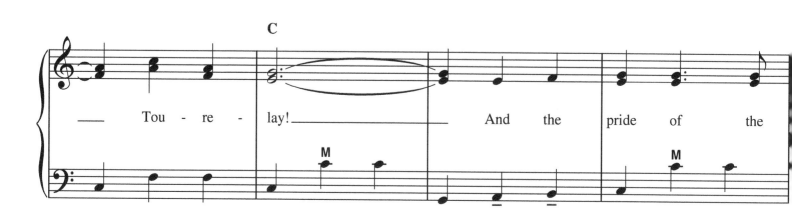

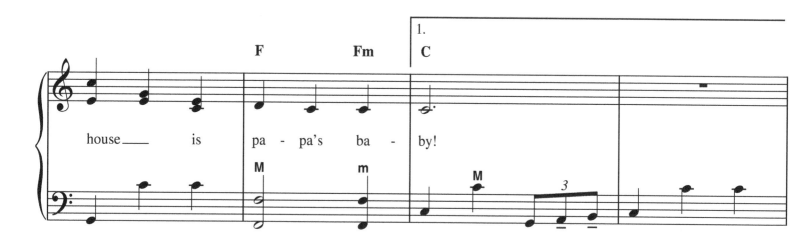

# THE WEARING OF THE GREEN

Eighteenth Century Irish Folksong

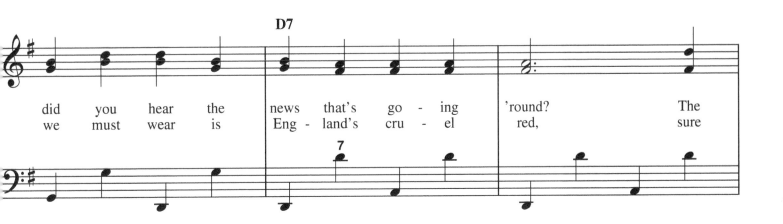

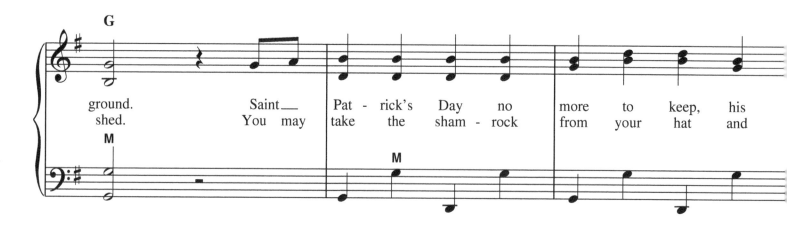

ground.
shed.
Saint___ Pat - rick's Day no more to keep, his
You may take the sham - rock from your hat and

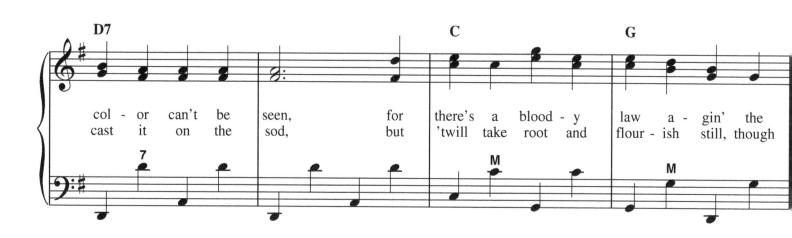

col - or can't be seen, for there's a blood - y law a - gin' the
cast it on the sod, but 'twill take root and flour - ish still, though

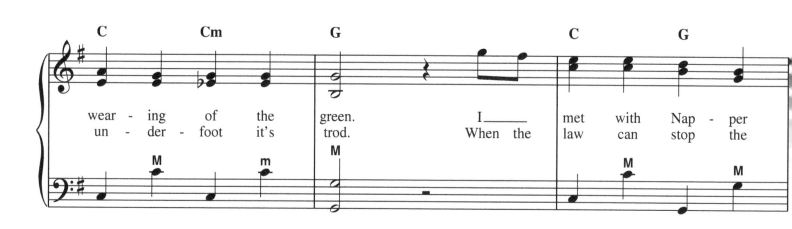

wear - ing of the green. I_____ met with Nap - per
un - der - foot it's trod. When the law can stop the

Tan - dy and he took me by the hand, and he
blades of grass from grow - ing as they grow, and___

# WHEN IRISH EYES ARE SMILING

Words by CHAUNCEY OLCOTT
and GEORGE GRAFF, JR.
Music by ERNEST R. BALL

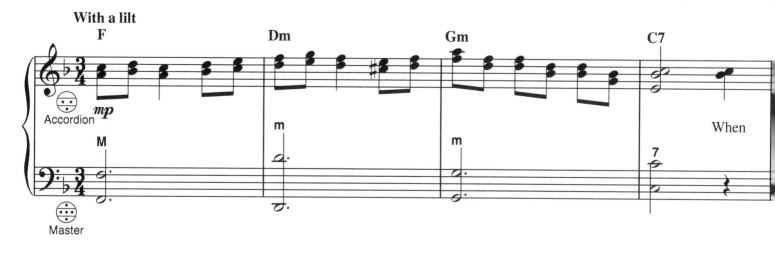

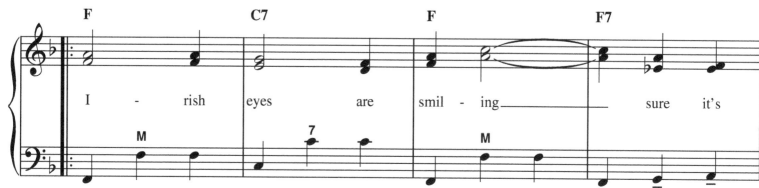

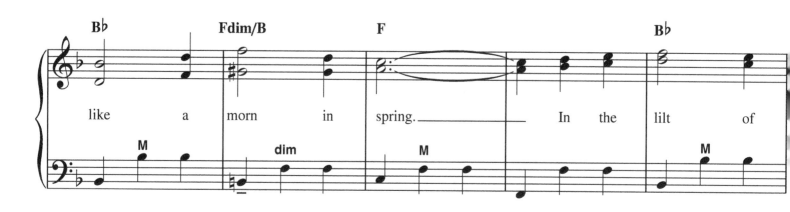

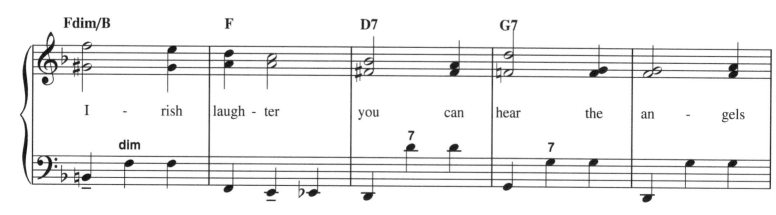

sing._____ When I - rish hearts are hap - py_____

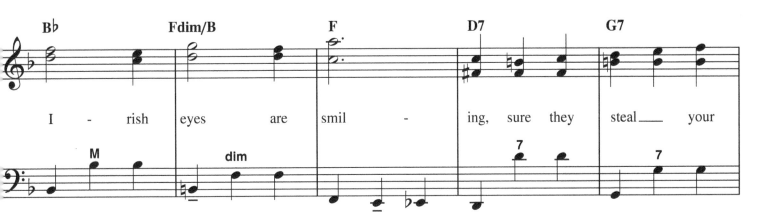

____ all the world seems bright and gay._____ And when

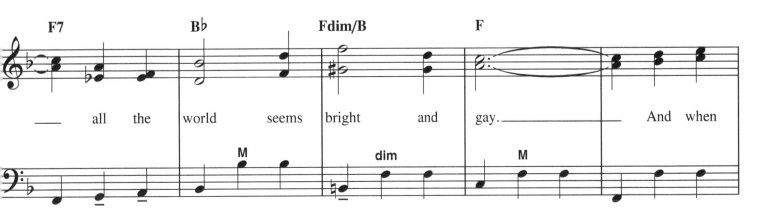

I - rish eyes are smil - ing, sure they steal____ your

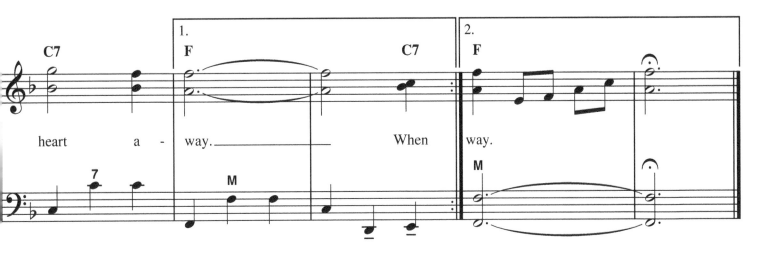

heart a - way._____ When way.

# A COLLECTION OF ALL-TIME FAVORITES
## FOR ACCORDION

### ACCORDION FAVORITES

*arr. Gary Meisner*

16 all-time favorites, arranged for accordion, including: Can't Smile Without You • Could I Have This Dance • Endless Love • Memory • Sunrise, Sunset • I.O.U. • and more.

00359012 .................................................................. $12.99

### ALL-TIME FAVORITES FOR ACCORDION

*arr. Gary Meisner*

20 must-know standards arranged for accordions. Includes: Ain't Misbehavin' • Autumn Leaves • Crazy • Hello, Dolly! • Hey, Good Lookin' • Moon River • Speak Softly, Love • Unchained Melody • The Way We Were • Zip-A-Dee-Doo-Dah • and more.

00311088 .................................................................. $10.95

### BROADWAY FAVORITES

*arr. Ken Kotwitz*

A collection of 17 wonderful show songs, including: Don't Cry for Me Argentina • Getting to Know You • If I Were a Rich Man • Oklahoma • People Will Say We're in Love • We Kiss in a Shadow.

00490157 .................................................................. $10.99

### THE CHRISTMAS ACCORDION SONGBOOK

*arr. Gary Meisner*

20 popular holiday songs arranged for accordion, including: Caroling, Caroling • Have Yourself a Merry Little Christmas • The Little Drummer Boy • Silver Bells • This Christmas • White Christmas • and more.

00146980 .................................................................. $9.99

### CHRISTMAS SONGS FOR ACCORDION

17 holiday hits, including: The Chipmunk Song • Frosty the Snow Man • A Holly Jolly Christmas • Jingle-Bell Rock • Pretty Paper • Rudolph the Red-Nosed Reindeer.

00359477 .................................................................. $8.99

### DISNEY SONGS FOR ACCORDION – 3RD EDITION

13 Disney favorites, including: Be Our Guest • Can You Feel the Love Tonight • Chim Chim Cher-ee • It's a Small World • Let It Go • Under the Sea • A Whole New World • You'll Be in My Heart • and more!

00152508 .................................................................. $12.99

### FRENCH SONGS FOR ACCORDION

*arr. Gary Meisner*

A très magnifique collection of 17 French standards arranged for the accordion. Includes: Autumn Leaves • Beyond the Sea • C'est Magnifique • I Love Paris • La Marseillaise • Let It Be Me (Je T'appartiens) • Under Paris Skies • Watch What Happens • and more.

00311498 .................................................................. $9.99

### ITALIAN SONGS FOR ACCORDION

*arr. Gary Meisner*

17 favorite Italian standards arranged for accordion, including: Carnival of Venice • Ciribiribin • Come Back to Sorrento • Funiculi, Funicula • La donna è mobile • La Spagnola • 'O Sole Mio • Santa Lucia • Tarantella • and more.

00311089 .................................................................. $9.95

### LATIN FAVORITES FOR ACCORDION

*arr. Gary Meisner*

20 Latin favorites, including: Bésame Mucho (Kiss Me Much) • The Girl from Ipanema • How Insensitive (Insensatez) • Perfidia • Spanish Eyes • So Nice (Summer Samba) • and more.

00310932 .................................................................. $10.99

### THE FRANK MAROCCO ACCORDION SONGBOOK

This songbook includes arrangements and recordings of 15 standards and original songs from legendary jazz accordionist Frank Marocco, including: All the Things You Are • Autumn Leaves • Beyond the Sea • Moon River • Moonlight in Vermont • Stormy Weather (Keeps Rainin' All the Time) • and more!

00233441   Book/Online Audio.................................................$19.99

### POLKA FAVORITES

*arr. Kenny Kotwitz*

An exciting new collection of 16 songs, including: Beer Barrel Polka • Liechtensteiner Polka • My Melody of Love • Paloma Blanca • Pennsylvania Polka • Too Fat Polka • and more.

00311573 .................................................................. $10.95

### STAR WARS FOR ACCORDION

A dozen songs from the *Star Wars* franchise: The Imperial March (Darth Vader's Theme) • Luke and Leia • March of the Resistance • Princess Leia's Theme • Rey's Theme • Star Wars (Main Theme) • and more.

00157380 .................................................................. $12.99

### LAWRENCE WELK'S POLKA FOLIO

More than 50 famous polkas, schottisches and waltzes arranged for piano and accordion, including: Blue Eyes • Budweiser Polka • Clarinet Polka • Cuckoo Polka • The Dove Polka • Draw One Polka • Gypsy Polka • Helena Polka • International Waltzes • Let's Have Another One • Schnitzelbank • Shuffle Schottische • Squeeze Box Polka • Waldteuful Waltzes • and more.

00123218 .................................................................. $12.99

**HAL•LEONARD®**

Visit Hal Leonard Online at
**www.halleonard.com**

0818
129